Violin Music the Whole World Loves

39 popular melodies
arranged for violin and piano
in the first position
for easy sight-reading
and
amusement in the home

By

C. Paul Herfurth

and

Edward Strietel

THE WILLIS MUSIC COMPANY

W. M. Co. 5744

CLASSIFIED INDEX

(The contents of this book has been arranged in alphabetical
order by title to facilitate finding a piece quickly)

FOREWORD

This book will prove an invaluable collection for all who have acquired a limited technique and who, for lack of time, wish to intensify the melody hour in the home with pieces they can play.

Also for the younger generation who—as all do—desire a short cut to sight-reading. The secret of sight-reading is simple: READ! READ! READ! To quote an eminent authority, Mr. Ernest Hutcheson, dean of the Juilliard School of Music, New York, viz:

> 'The greatest mistake that students make is the breaking away from "assignments" and the reading of music that is technically far too difficult for them. The result is discouraging because, since their fingers are not ready to perform the intricacies before them, the work of coördinating eye and brain is slowed up. Music of one's own grade should be read. If possible music should be bought in volumes rather than in single sheets.'

Hence, if you wish to read with facility: READ, READ, READ, music within your ability and read it as much as you do books, magazines, or newspapers.

First: Glance through the piece you are about to play and judge what is expected of your fingers. Then: Begin to play in a slow tempo. Do not hesitate, keep the tempo; even if you make mistakes.

L. B. E.

America, the Beautiful

Tune "Materna" by
SAMUEL A. WARD
Arr. by C. Paul Herfurth

Aria
from the Opera "Der Freischütz"

CARL MARIA VON WEBER
(1786-1826)
Arr. by C. Paul Herfurth

W.M.Co.5744-Comp.

Adeste Fideles

Portuguese Hymn
Arr. by EDWARD STRIETEL

Annie Laurie
(Scotch Tune)

LADY JOHN SCOTT
(1847)
Arr. by EDWARD STRIETEL

Auld Lang Syne

Scotch Folk-song
Arr. by EDWARD STRIETEL

Battle Hymn of the Republic

Arr. by EDWARD STRIETEL

Written about 1855 by
WILLIAM STEFFE
A Southern composer of Sunday School Songs

W.M.Co. 5744-Comp.

Beautiful Dreamer

STEPHEN C. FOSTER
(1826-1864)
Arr. by C. Paul Herfurth

Beautiful Heaven
(Cielito Lindo)

Mexican Folk-song
Arr. by C. Paul Herfurth

W.M.Co. 5744 - Comp.

Carry Me Back to Old Virginny

JAMES A. BLAND
Arr. by C. Paul Herfurth

Columbia, the Gem of the Ocean

English Melody
Arr. by EDWARD STRIETEL

Come back to Erin

CLARIBEL
CHARLOTTE ARLINGTON BARNARD
(1830-1869)
Arr. by EDWARD STRIETEL

Comin' thro' the Rye

(Scotch Air)

Arr. by EDWARD STRIETEL

W. M. Co. 5744 - Comp.

Dixie Land

(Song of the Confederacy)

Written in 1859 for a minstrel show by
DAN D. EMMETT
(1815-1904)

Arr. by EDWARD STRIETEL

W.M.Co.5744-Comp.

Hail, Columbia
(Written during the threatened war with France in 1798)

Attributed to PHILIP PYLE (_ 1793)
Arr. by EDWARD STRIETEL

The Heart Bowed Down
from "The Bohemian Girl"

MICH. Wm BALFE
(1808-1870)
Arr. by EDWARD STRIETEL

W. M. Co. 5744 - Comp.

Home on the Range

Cowboy Song
Arr. by C. Paul Herfurth

Home, Sweet Home

HENRY R. BISHOP
(1786-1855)
Arr. by EDWARD STRIETEL

Juanita*

Old Spanish Melody
Arr. by EDWARD STRIETEL

* Pronounced, Wa-nee-tah

W. M. Co. 5744 - Comp.

Copyright, MCMXIV, by The Willis Music Company

'Tis the last Rose of Summer
(Irish Air)

Melody used by
Fried. Flotow in the opera "Martha"
Arr. by EDWARD STRIETEL

Listen to the Mocking-Bird

ALICE HAWTHORNE
pseudonym for Septimus Winner
Arr. by EDWARD STRIETEL

W. M. Co. 5744 - Comp.

Lorelei

FRIEDRICH SILCHER
(1789-1860)
Arr. by EDWARD STREITEL

Copyright, *MCMXIV, by The Willis Music Company*

Long, Long Ago

THOMAS H. BAYLY
(1797-1839)
Arr. by C. Paul Herfurth

Marseillaise
French National Anthem

Written for Luckner's Army
as it marched on the Tuileries
Aug. 10, 1792

Arr. by EDWARD STRIETEL

ROUGET DE LISLE

W. M. C o. 5744 - Comp.

Massa's in de Cold, Cold Ground

STEPHEN C. FOSTER
(1826-1864)
Arr. by EDWARD STRIETEL

My Country, 'tis of Thee

First sung publicly at a children's celebration
of American Independence, Boston, July, 4, 1852

HENRY CAREY (1685-1743)
Arr. by EDWARD STRIETEL

My Old Kentucky Home

STEPHEN C. FOSTER
(1826-1864)
Arr. by EDWARD STRIETEL

Old Black Joe

STEPHEN C. FOSTER
(1826-1864)
Arr. by EDWARD STRIETEL

W. M.Co. 5744 - Comp.

The Old Folks at Home

STEPHEN C. FOSTER
(1826-1864)
Arr. by EDWARD STRIETEL

Copyright, MCMXIV, by The Willis Music Company

O Sanctissima
(O Thou Joyful Day)

Latin hymn A.D. 1500
Folk-song of the Sicilian Seas
F. GRÜBER

Arr. by EDWARD STRIETEL

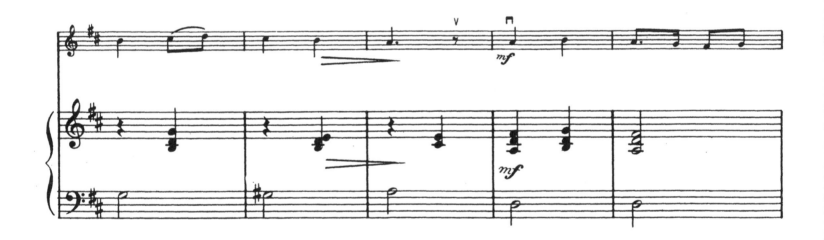

W.M.Co. 5744-Comp.

Rock of Ages

THOMAS HASTINGS
Arr. by EDWARD STRIETEL

2664 - 3 W

Santa Lucia

Neapolitan Boat Song
Arr. by C. Paul Herfurth

Silent Night, Holy Night

FRANZ GRÜBER
(1818)
Arr. by EDWARD STRIETEL

The Star-Spangled Banner

THE NATIONAL ANTHEM
Written during the war of 1812

Melody "To Anacreon in Heaven"
By JOHN STAFFORD SMITH (1750-1836)
Arr. by EDWARD STRIETEL

Silver Threads among the Gold

H. P. DANKS
(1834-1903)
Arr. by C. Paul Herfurth

W. M. Co. 5744 - Comp

Songs My Mother Taught Me

ANTON DVOŘÁK
(1841-1904)
Arr. by C. Paul Herfurth

W.M.Co. 5744-Comp.

Song of the Volga Boatmen

Russian Folk-song
Arr. by C. Paul Herfurth

Turkey in the Straw

American Folk-tune
Arr. by C. Paul Herfurth

W. M. Co. 5744 - Comp.

D.S. 𝄋 to ⊕ then Coda

CODA

Wearing of the Green

An old revolutionary street ballad
used in the play,"Arrah na Pogue"

DION BOUCICAULT
Arr. by EDWARD STRIETEL

Yankee Doodle

During the Revolutionary War this song was used by the British to make fun of the Yankees and later by the Yankees to taunt the British.

Source unknown
Arr. by EDWARD STRIETEL

Copyright, MCMXIV, by The Willis Music Company